Our Guests

Cover Image by Thomas Kinkade

HARVEST HOUSE PUBLISHERS
Eugene, Oregon 97402

Cover Image: "Home Is Where the Heart Is" by Thomas Kinkade

Simpler Times Guest Book

Copyright © 1997 Thomas Kinkade, Media Arts Group, Inc., San Jose, CA

ISBN 1-56507-614-1

The cover image is copyrighted by Thomas Kinkade and may not be copied or reproduced without the artist's permission. For information regarding Thomas Kinkade art prints, collectibles and other products, please contact:

Media Arts Group, Inc.
521 Charcot Avenue
San Jose, CA 95131
1-800-366-3733

Cover design by Koechel Peterson & Associates, Minneapolis, Minnesota

Scripture quotations are from The Holy Bible, New International Version® Copyright © 1973, 1978, 1984 by the International Bible Society. Used by permission of Zondervan Publishing House.

Printed in the United States of America.

97 98 99 99 00 01 02 / IP / 10 9 8 7 6 5 4 3

Someone asked me once why I paint so many
houses and cottages with warm, glowing windows. I
paint glowing windows because glowing windows say
home to me. Glowing windows say welcome. They say
all is well, that someone's waiting, someone cares
enough to turn the lights on. As I am dabbing brushfuls
of golden paint on those windows, I am always
imagining a world of intimate gatherings, of quiet times
spent in the company of loved ones.

Your home is your welcoming world. It is your anchor,
the resting place for your heart. Times together with
friends and family are what put the glow in your
windows. May you and all who enter your home enjoy
much warmth inside.

Thomas Kinkade

The beginning, I hope, of many joyful days!

Dombey and Son

Date   *Guests*

Date   _Guests_

Date *Guests*

Date   *Guests*

Date   *Guests*

Date   *Guests*

Home

Is where you can be silent
and still be heard.
Where you can ask and find out
who you are.
Where people laugh with you
about yourself.
Where sorrow is divided
and joy multiplied.
Where we share and love and grow.

❧

Author Unknown

Date   *Guests*

Date   *Guests*

Date   *Guests*

Date   Guests

Date   *Guests*

Date   *Guests*

Date   *Guests*

Date   *Guests*

Date   Guests

────────

You are as welcome in my home
as you are in my heart.

Jeanne Sheridan

Date   *Guests*

Date   *Guests*

Date   *Guests*

Date   *Guests*

Date   Guests

Date　　　*Guests*

Lord, this humble house we'd keep
Sweet with play and calm with sleep.
Help us so that we may give
Beauty to the lives we live.
Let Thy love and let Thy grace
Shine upon our dwelling place.

❦

Edgar Guest

Date   Guests

Date   Guests

Date   _Guests_

Date   *Guests*

Date   *Guests*

Date   *Guests*

Date   Guests

Date   Guests

Date   Guests

_____ _____

_____ _____

_____ _____

_____ _____

_____ _____

_____ _____

_____ _____

What is more agreeable than one's home?

Cicero

Date　　　*Guests*

Date   *Guests*

Date *Guests*

Date   *Guests*

Date   *Guests*

Date   Guests

By wisdom a house is built,
and through understanding it is established;
through knowledge its rooms are filled
with rare and beautiful treasures.

❧

Proverbs 24:3,4

Date   *Guests*

Date   *Guests*

Date　　　Guests

Date   _Guests_

Date   Guests

Date   *Guests*

Date   Guests

Date   Guests

Date   Guests

_____   _____

_____   _____

_____   _____

_____   _____

_____   _____

_____   _____

❧❧

A home is made from love,
warm as the golden hearthfire on the floor.

Author Unknown

❧❧

Date   Guests

Date   *Guests*

Date   Guests

Date   *Guests*

Date　　　Guests

Date   _Guests_

A house is built of logs and stone,
Of tiles and posts and piers;
A home is built of loving deeds
That stand a thousand years.

❧

Victor Hugo

Date   Guests

Date   *Guests*

Date　　　　Guests

Date   *Guests*

Date   _Guests_

Date   Guests

Date　　　*Guests*

Date   *Guests*

Date   *Guests*

Offer hospitality to one another.

1 Peter 4:9

Date   *Guests*

Date　　　Guests

Date   *Guests*

Date   Guests

Date　　Guests

Date   *Guests*

The beauty of the house is order,
The blessing of the house is contentment,
The glory of the house is hospitality.

❧

Author Unknown

Date Guests

Date   *Guests*

Date   *Guests*

Date   *Guests*

Date   *Guests*

Date　　*Guests*

Date   *Guests*

Date   Guests

Date   *Guests*

Weary Traveller,
Rest ye here beside our hearth,
And fill your soul with meat and mirth.

Author Unknown

Date   *Guests*

Date   Guests

Date   Guests

Date   Guests

Date   *Guests*

Date   Guests

Date   *Guests*

Date   *Guests*

Date   Guests

Date   *Guests*

Home is where the heart is,
The soul's bright guiding star.
Home is where real love is,
Where our own dear ones are.
Home means someone waiting,
To give a welcome smile.
Home means peace and joy and rest
And everything worthwhile.

❧

Author Unknown